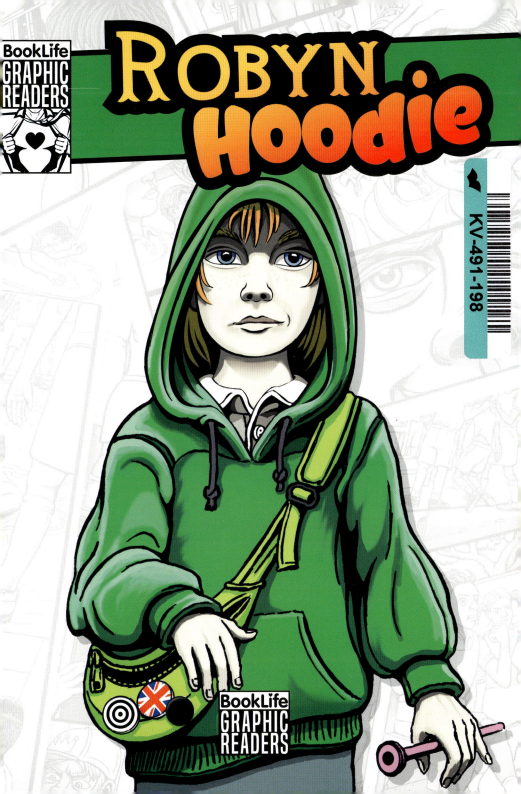

HOW TO READ A COMIC BOOK

Comic books are made up of pictures in boxes, called panels. Look at each of these panels from left to right, and top to bottom.

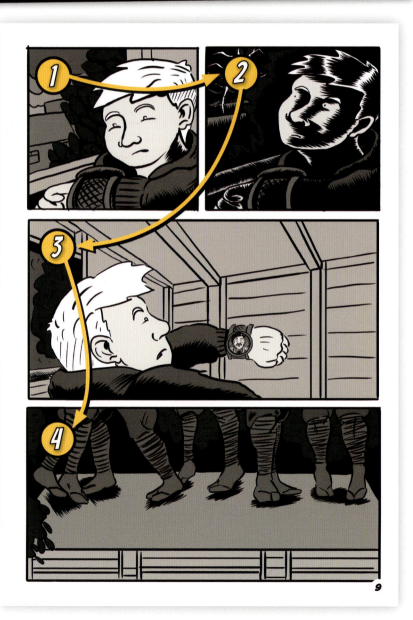

Read the speech bubbles, caption boxes and any sound effects from left to right, too. Together with the images, these will tell you the story.

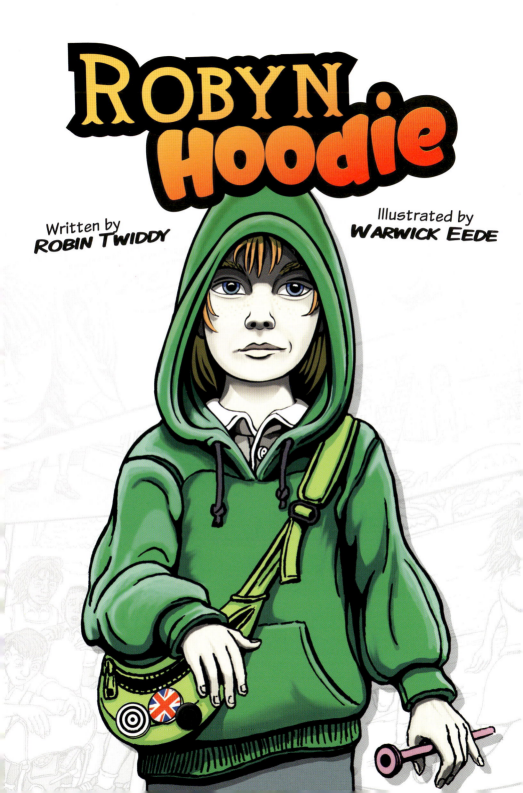

9

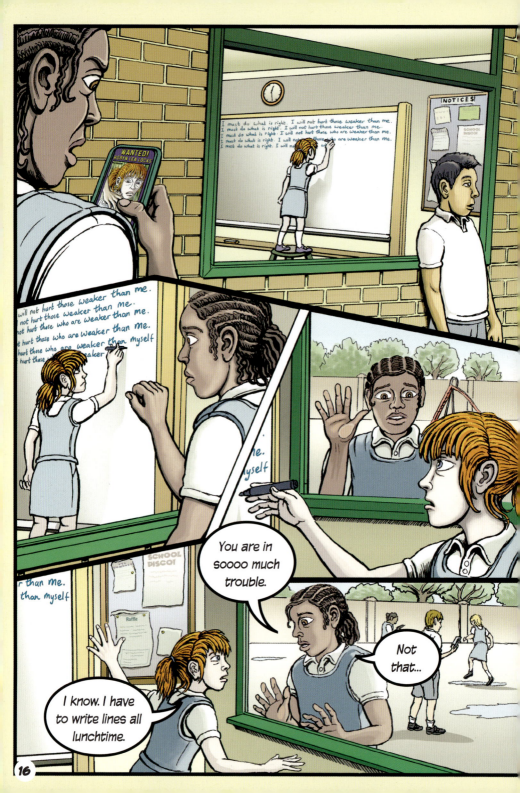

That was when I first met Robyn.

Right, we made a dent in the King's armour. Now we deliver the killing blow! Here's what we do...

Robyn laid her plan out for us.

And we did what she asked.

We talked to every kid on the playground.

The King had no idea what was coming.

Like flies to honey.

@2023 BookLife Publishing Ltd.
King's Lynn, Norfolk PE30 4LS

ISBN 978-1-80505-007-0

All rights reserved. Printed in China.
A catalogue record for this book is
available from the British Library.

Robyn Hoodie
Written by Robin Twiddy
Illustrated by Warwick Eede

ABOUT BOOKLIFE GRAPHIC READERS

BookLife Graphic Readers are designed to encourage reluctant readers to take the next step in their reading adventure. These books are a perfect accompaniment to the BookLife Readers phonics scheme and are designed to be read by children who have a good grasp on reading but are reluctant to pick up a full-prose book. Graphic Readers combine graphic and prose storytelling in a way that aids comprehension and presents a more accessible reading experience for reluctant readers and lovers of comic books.

ABOUT THE AUTHOR

Robin is a lifelong comic book fan whose love for the medium led to it being the topic of his undergraduate dissertation. He is the author of many great BookLife titles, including several entries into the BookLife phonic reader scheme. Robin loves action, adventure and humour and brings these elements together into exciting narratives you won't forget.

ABOUT THE ILLUSTRATOR

Warwick Eede illustrates from his home in Lincolnshire. He also works as a part-time Grammar school Art teacher. He loves chilling with the family and eating lasagne while listening to the Ramones. His favourite film is Jaws.